trotman

REAL LIFE ISSUES:
COPING WITH LIFE

KT-228-059

Jonathan Bradley

Real Life Issues: Coping with Life
This first edition published in 2005 by Trotman and Company Ltd
2 The Green, Richmond, Surrey TW9 1PL

© Trotman and Company Limited 2005

Editorial and Publishing Team
Author Jonathan Bradley
Editorial Mina Patria, Editorial Director; Rachel Lockhart, Commissioning Editor;
Catherine Travers, Managing Editor; Bianca Knights, Assistant Editor
Production Ken Ruskin, Head of Pre-press and Production;
James Rudge, Production Artworker
Sales and Marketing Deborah Jones, Head of Sales and Marketing
Advertising Tom Lee, Commercial Director
Managing Director Toby Trotman

Designed by XAB

British Library Cataloguing in Publication Data
A catalogue record for this book is available from the British Library

ISBN 0 85660 994 3

All rights reserved. No part of this publication may be reproduced, stored in a
retrieval system or transmitted in any form or by any means, electronic and
mechanical, photocopying, recording or otherwise without prior permission
of Trotman and Company Ltd.

Typeset by Tradespools Publishing Solutions
Printed and bound in Great Britain by
Cromwell Press, Trowbridge, Wiltshire

CONTENTS:

'A natural part of coping is to be able to respond to changes.'

REAL LIFE ISSUES:
Coping with Life

ABOUT THE AUTHOR

Jonathan Bradley has worked as a Child and Adolescent
Psychotherapist in the NHS for a number of years. At present he works
in the Adolescent Department at the Tavistock Clinic, an internationally
famous clinic and training institution for therapists. Before becoming a
psychotherapist he taught adolescents. He lives in London with his
family, which includes teenage children.

REAL LIFE ISSUES:
Coping with Life

ACKNOWLEDGEMENTS

Thank you to those who have contributed their experiences to this volume; to my reviewers, Carys, Owen and Rosie; and to colleagues and friends for thoughts about the contents.

INTRODUCTION
Recognising the rules that can help you cope with life

This book will help you to think about the many changes and pressures in life that can sometimes seem too much to deal with. Some of these changes and pressures come from inside ourselves (eg you might set very high standards for yourself) and others come from outside (eg exams, life changes). How is it possible to avoid being overwhelmed? Is it possible to enjoy life when it is so demanding? This book looks at the ordinary issues of teenage life – family, school, friendships, sexuality. You will find some general rules about coping, rules that can be remembered and applied to different aspects of life.

HOW ARE YOU? HOW AM I?

We've all heard this question many times: 'How are you?'

There are plenty of ways of answering it:

- 'Fine'
- 'Not bad'
- 'Well, am I pleased to see you!' (followed by a lengthy conversation)
- 'Fine, thanks' (not followed by a conversation of any kind!)
- A shrug (followed by another shrug if necessary).

These questions and answers take place many times a day. Sometimes they don't mean much – they are just meant as a social greeting. At other times it can be very important to know that someone is interested enough to ask how we are. At times another person's interest may not be wanted, and may seem like more than we can cope with. But, welcome or not, asking 'How are you?' or – when asking questions about yourself – 'How am I?' needs to be a regular part of life, a way of checking on ourselves, sometimes on our own, but often with the help of others.

Checklist for coping

We'll look more closely at these 'rules' later in the book, but for the moment here are some useful questions; if you ask yourself these questions then you can use them as a checklist for coping.

Checklist questions	More information...
☐ **Are you adaptable?** Do you manage to think about new situations and adopt a flexible approach, or do you find it difficult to change your mind? Do you get caught up in routines that can't be changed?	See Chapter 1
☐ **Are you resilient?** What happens to you when something goes badly? Do you give up, or can you bounce back?	See Chapter 1
☐ **Do you have positive relationships with those around you?** What company do you keep? Do you have good friends? Are you able to hold on to a sense of your own individuality, or do you get lost in the crowd? Are you involved in a friendship that is not good for you? How do you relate to adults?	See Chapters 2–4

Checklist questions	More information...

☐ **Do you have self-regard?**
See Chapter 5
Are you in touch with your personal
history? Are you kind in the way you
think about yourself? Or are you very
self-critical – too harsh with yourself?

☐ **Can you get by without needing
emotional 'crutches'?**
See Chapter 6
Are you able to manage day by day,
or do you need drugs (eg alcohol,
cigarettes, illegal drugs) to help you
get through?

☐ **Are you able to use your mind?**
See Chapter 7
Everyone has a mind, but thinking
can sometimes be painful. Does your
mind help you to think things through,
or do you give up and stop thinking
about situations?

☐ **Are you aware of your own feelings?**
See Chapter 7
Are you able to let your own feelings
come to the surface, to be aware of them
and express them when appropriate?
Or do you get embarrassed, push
feelings down or pretend they are not
there?

HOW DO YOU RATE?

Try the exercises on the next page. You should find them useful,
particularly as the book develops.

EXERCISE ONE: 'HOW AM I?'

How do you rate yourself on a scale of 1 to 5? (Score yourself 5 for most positive outlook and 1 for most negative.)

Category	1	2	3	4	5
1. Adaptability					
2. Resilience					
3. Relationships					
4. Self-regard					
5. Emotional crutches					
6. Use of mind					
7. In touch with feelings					

FINDINGS

Add up your overall score. If you gave yourself a score near the maximum (35), you are probably being too soft on yourself! If you gave yourself a score near the minimum (7), you are probably being too hard on yourself! Try it again. Look at the pattern of your score.

EXERCISE TWO: 'HOW ARE YOU?'

This exercise is exactly the same, except this time you need to ask a friend to rate you. Ask your friend for a total score, and also for the score under each category.

Category	1	2	3	4	5
1. Adaptability					
2. Resilience					
3. Relationships					
4. Self-regard					
5. Emotional crutches					
6. Use of mind					
7. In touch with feelings					

What did you score highly on, and what did you score poorly on? Do the results surprise you?

MAKING SENSE OF THE SCORES

See how the 'How am I?' and 'How are you?' scores compare – look at both the totals and the pattern of scores.

Totals

1 If the totals in both exercises are within 5 points of each other, then you probably have a perceptive friend and are good at letting yourself be 'seen' by others. (Whether or not this is so depends on the patterns within the score. Even if the overall totals were similar, how similar were the individual scores for each category?)

2 If the totals are more than 15 points apart, ask yourself if you think your friend is really interested in doing the exercise for you. (See the different ways of saying 'how are you?' above.) If he or she *is* genuinely interested in helping, then look at the pattern of the score and see where the scores were different.

Patterns

It is very interesting to see how your own scores in each of the seven categories compare with the scores your friend gave you.

1 If you both arrived at the same total score but your friend gave you higher or lower scores in each category than you did yourself, they may not know you as well as you thought.

2 Did your own rating and that of your friend come close in four or more categories? This is impressive, and it shows how it is possible to be known well by someone else. (And if you do need to talk to someone, it can help to know that this person has an accurate view of you.)

3 Were your scores very different? If so, remember that this is a 'fun' exercise and that there can be many reasons, not connected with you, why this might have happened.

We'll return often to the checklist given on page 2 throughout the book. You may find it useful to do the exercises above again later, after you have thought more about each of the checkpoints.

WHY IS THIS BOOK IMPORTANT?

Coping with life is something that, like it or not, everyone has to do! It is very important to think about ways of dealing with the problems life can throw at us, and to learn how to know ourselves.

There is also evidence to suggest that it is harder to cope now (particularly if you are a teenager) than it ever has been.

Some facts

Life has become more complicated for everyone in recent years, and teenagers are no exception. Some recent studies have illustrated this:

FACT BOX

'The rate of emotional problems such as anxiety and depression has increased by 70% among adolescents.'
Source: 'Time Trends in Adolescent Mental Health', Madeleine Bunting, the *Guardian*, 13 September 2004)

The article quoted above is based on a study conducted in Britain, which looked at three generations of 15-year-olds in 1974, 1986 and 1999. It showed that behavioural problems had worsened steadily since 1974, but emotional issues had really changed only since 1986. Tom Wylie, Chief Executive of the National Youth Agency, commented that 'transitions to adulthood are not just longer, they are also reversible – teenagers move out of the family to take a job but it doesn't work out and they have to move back home. All of that turbulence has become sharper.'

FACT BOX

'According to a survey carried out by Bliss magazine/the Guardian, half of teenage girls say they cannot cope with the pressures of modern life; 90% have felt depressed and 42% feel low regularly.'

Source: *The Week*, 5 March 2005

Coping, or not coping, is in the news at the moment, and there is much anxiety about what might be going wrong for some people – though not everyone finds life difficult all the time, of course. Should adults feel guilty about what a difficult world they hand over to adolescents, or should teenagers feel guilty about their behaviour?

The one thing that is for certain is that, if you sometimes feel like things are too much and you can't cope, you can be sure that you are not alone.

'... if you sometimes feel like things are too much and you can't cope, you can be sure that you are not alone.'

What is 'coping'?

If you look up 'coping' in a dictionary, it will probably talk about dealing successfully with a situation or problem and keeping things under control. This book will mention 'coping' quite a lot – and in the context of life in general, coping is a lot more complicated. Consider the following example:

JANE'S STORY

Jane was only 16 when her father died after a long illness. The family had been expecting it but even so it was a massive shock, especially since daily routines had for a long time been organised to take account of her father's illness. Jane felt that her father's death had left her numb. She expected to be much sadder and she felt very guilty that she was more concerned about preparing for her GCSEs, which were coming up soon. Friends and school were very sympathetic, and she was offered counselling. She thought that this might be helpful later but she felt very strongly that she had to put things out of her mind and focus on her work, which became very important to her. In fact, she coped well with her preparation and the exams themselves. Afterwards it was a different story, and she collapsed under the strain of what she had had to go through. Her family and friends had been waiting for this to happen and were at hand to provide her with the help she needed.

Jane's story shows that:

1. 'Coping' doesn't mean being happy and perfect! Jane had to cope with the stress of exams, at the same time as having to cope with the loss of her father.
2. Part of being able to cope depends on knowing quite a lot about yourself. Jane knew that the best way to manage the exams was to promise herself that afterwards she could allow herself to 'collapse'.

3 Coping with life is about coping *overall, most of the time*. It is inevitable that there will be times when you feel you're not coping very well.

SUMMARY

In this Introduction we have touched on the idea that to cope with life we need to know ourselves. The checklist on page 2 gave you an opportunity to start thinking about the different attitudes and skills that can help, and the seven different points it covered will each be explored further in this book. The first two points, adaptability and resilience, are explored in Chapter 1.

CHAPTER ONE:

ALL CHANGE!
How to manage when everything feels confused

When most people think of adolescence they think of things changing. This chapter looks at ways of coping and adapting to the different kinds of change that happen throughout life, particularly during the teenage years.

CHANGES IN ADOLESCENCE

- Physical development – change in body image.
- Sexual development and preoccupation with sexual identity.
- Development of emotional maturity – from child to adult.
- Development of relationships.
- Increase in external pressures eg taking exams.
- Development of plans and ambitions for the future.
- Increase in time spent socialising.
- Possible development of issues about drugs.

This list does not include everything: you may be able to add others. However, it does show that an awful lot of things change very quickly during adolescence. But even though it's easy to make a list, it can be more difficult to deal with change.

Recognising change

If we are in the middle of something while it's changing, it is difficult to recognise what is happening. For example, the earth is moving all the time. It is in orbit around the sun at an enormous speed of over 60,000 miles an hour – but we don't feel a thing, because we are on it as it is moving; we are moving with it. (It is quite a thought, though, to imagine ourselves spinning through space like that!)

As it moves around the sun on its annual circuit, the earth is also rotating. It takes 24 hours to go through one revolution, but it turns very slowly at the top and bottom and much quicker in the middle, a bit like a spinning top.

What does this tell us about change in general?

1 Change may be happening much more quickly than we imagine!
2 Change happens to us all – but at different speeds, so it seems that some people have to travel a lot further than others to get to the same place.

How do we cope with change when we are not aware of it happening?

In the Introduction to this book we looked at a checklist for coping. The first question was on Adaptability. It asked:

❑ **Are you adaptable?**
Do you manage to think about new situations and adopt a flexible approach, or do you find it difficult to change your mind? Do you get caught up in routines that can't be changed?

Adaptability means the ability to fit or adjust yourself to different situations – to alter your plans or modify your expectations in response to something you had not anticipated. Adaptability is rather a dreary word. Try thinking of it like this: at a football match I overheard a football coach, absolutely desperate because his team were losing 4-0, call out to his dozy defenders: 'Expect the unexpectable!' Although you won't find the word 'unexpectable' in the dictionary, the advice seemed to work because they did better after that (though they still lost).

The pace of change in your body

It is difficult to prepare for something if you don't know when it will happen or how long it will last.

Just try to count up the number of times a relation has looked at you in amazement and commented on how tall you are or what big feet you have. People really are amazed to find how much you have changed since they last saw you.

Consider how quickly things can change. Ian was 5 foot 2 inches (1.57 metres) tall when he was 12 years old. A year later he was 5 foot 7 inches (1.70 metres). That is a growth rate of over 8% in one year. Perhaps 8% does not seem much, but let's look at what would happen if that pace of growth (five inches / 13 centimetres a year) continued:

Age	Height (feet' inches")	Height (metres)
12	5'2"	1.57
13	5'7"	1.70
14	6'0"	1.83
15	6'5"	1.96
16	6'10"	2.09
17	7'3"	2.22
18	7'8"	2.35

Very few people grow to be 7 foot 8 inches (2.35 metres) tall! The table above shows that the rate of growth we experience during adolescence simply can't last for long. In fact, it could be over in a year or two, though there are usually more gradual phases of growth before and after the fast phase.

Expected and unexpected change

The kind of change that we can't recognise because we are in the middle of it, or that we have to wait for, not knowing when it will happen, is the most difficult kind of change to manage. It is easier to face up to something when we know what it is and when it will happen. The list at the beginning of this chapter summarised the broad areas of change. Let's look at them again, but this time try to describe them in terms of whether we can predict how and when they will occur.

'The kind of change that we have to wait for, not knowing when it will happen, is the most difficult kind of change to manage.'

Type of change	Can we predict when it will happen?
Physical change	No
Body image	No
Emotional change	No
Sexual development	No
Developing relationships	No
Taking exams	Yes
Plans and ambitions	No
Socialising	No
Issues about drugs	No

Only one of the types of change listed above can be predicted accurately. We know that all the others *will* happen, but we don't know *when*. This is not the way we would want it in an ideal world. In general, people like their lives to be predictable and controllable. For example, we certainly would not buy a car on these terms – just imagine the car salesman saying: 'You have a good car here. Just sit in it, keep it topped up with petrol. Remember to keep your foot on the accelerator and, I promise you, one day it will suddenly decide to take off.' Can you imagine how stressful it would be, not knowing when the car might suddenly spring to life!

SEXUAL DEVELOPMENT AND SEXUAL IDENTITY

Thoughts and feelings about sexuality are very important throughout our lives. In this section of the chapter we'll look at this from the point of view of the changes that happen during adolescence. Chapter 2 will discuss friendship and relationships, taking a look at sexuality from another angle.

> **For a closer look at this issue,**
> **see *Real Life Issues: Sex & Relationships***

Unexpected thoughts about sexuality

New thoughts and feelings can arrive unexpectedly during adolescence and take you by surprise. You can even start to become interested in sexual issues without being properly aware that this is what is going on.

Our awareness of what's happening now is connected with our feelings about the past. The development of more adult sexual feelings often happens at the same time as the development of a more adult emotional viewpoint. This can mean 'dealing with' things which happened a long time ago and which may have been pushed aside and half-forgotten. Rachel's story shows how our past can become mixed up with the present.

RACHEL'S STORY

When she was 15, Rachel started to have disturbing dreams about her father who, in reality, had been absent from her life for many years, since she was a young girl. On waking, the dreams disturbed her, particularly since she would wake up feeling quite upset. It also confused her that at the same time she was getting interested in boys. What did this mean? Why dream of her father at this time and in this way?

In her case, when she managed to talk it through, it seemed that it was only now, when she was becoming interested in boys, that she could acknowledge some of the painful feelings associated with the departure of her father from her life. It was as if a younger, sensitive part of herself and an excited adolescent part were both announcing their presence at the same time! Living and feeling on two levels like this takes up a lot of energy.

Where we have come from and where we are going to

It is very common in adolescence to have strong feelings about most things, and this is particularly true of sexuality. It makes sense that this should happen. Entering puberty and developing an adult body makes a difference to our relationships. Your body is developing, looking to the future, but you may have feelings that seem as though they belong to someone much younger. You might feel that you want to hold on to your childhood for a bit longer. One aspect of your life is changing, but experiences and feelings that developed much earlier in your life are still foremost in your mind. This is true of Stephanie (see her story on page 25), whose deep friendship with Lucie enabled her

'Your body is developing, looking to the future, but you may have feelings that seem as though they belong to someone much younger.'

to move from one kind of relationship with her mother to one that was more appropriate to someone of her age.

This kind of double agenda can lead to very complicated feelings; particularly feelings associated with the time when we were very young and dependent on our parents or guardians. Our bodies and minds are developing so it's perfectly normal to feel confused about identity at this time, particularly our sexual identity.

During this time of our lives, boys can develop close, intense friendships with other boys, and girls with other girls. These friendships develop naturally between people of the same age who are trying to deal with feeling differently about themselves and their parents. To find out more about these close friendships, see the section in Chapter 2 on Close Friends.

It is quite normal to be worried about your sexuality, and to wonder whether you might be gay or lesbian. You might question how close you should be to someone of your own sex as you grow up. It is not surprising, especially if you start to feel that you don't know who you are.

In all the turmoil you might feel differently not only from day to day, but even from hour to hour – one moment you might think 'I am gay'; the next moment you might decide 'no, I'm not', then, five minutes later, change your mind and think 'yes, I am'. Each time you come to a different conclusion and each time you're sure you're right. Then you feel the opposite is true. The problem is that each thought is accompanied by very strong feelings. Try to keep in mind that just because a feeling is strong, that doesn't mean that it is permanent.

> If you have been feeling confused about your sexuality for a long time, and the feeling won't go away, there are organisations that you can contact to talk it over with someone – have a look at the Further Information section at the end of this book.

COPING WITH CONFUSION

So what is 'coping' when you're in this state of mind? You're getting many mixed messages from inside yourself, and you're probably having to deal with very strong emotions, too. You may be feeling anxious and stressed out. It is important to remember that this is a time of great change, and you will get through it! Remember that your feelings about many things – including yourself – can and will change.

Stress and how to cope with it

Waiting for something to happen is bound to lead to stress and anxiety.

As human beings we function better when we can recognise possible danger. From the list on page 13, for example, 'Taking exams' stands out from the others. It is possible to know when these will happen, and what you need to do to deal with them. Getting stressed in such situations is quite common, and it can actually make your mind sharper. It is difficult to stay sharp when we don't know when something will happen or how we are going to recognise it.

> **For a closer look at stress,**
> **see *Real Life Issues: Stress***

HOW TO COPE WITH GENERAL ANXIETY

■ Try to look at the specifics rather than letting a general cloud of worry hang over you.

■ Try to pinpoint the facts of the matter. These may not be as difficult to find out as first appears, even when you are right in the middle of everything. With practice it is possible to look at ourselves from an 'outside' perspective – to find out more about how to do this, see Chapter 7.

■ Keep in contact with your friends.

CAREFUL OBSERVATION

Another important way of making sure stress and worry don't get out of control is to make sure you are able to observe yourself and make a judgment about how things are really going. The checklist in the Introduction asked two questions relating to observation:

❏ **Are you able to use your mind?**

Everyone has a mind, but thinking can sometimes be painful. Does your mind help you to think things through, or do you give up and stop thinking about situations?

❏ **Are you aware of your own feelings?**

Are you able to let your own feelings come to the surface, to be aware of them and express them when appropriate? Or do you get embarrassed, push feelings down or pretend they are not there?

Being able to do these things will really help you cope. Thinking things through and making sure you understand and show your feelings makes it more likely that you will be able to keep things under control.

TIP BOX

By thinking and feeling it is possible to become more aware of changes as they happen. Sometimes this can involve learning painful but worthwhile things about ourselves. For more information on thinking and feeling, see Chapter 5 (Self-regard) and Chapter 7 (Using your mind and your feelings).

MARY'S STORY

Mary had had a pattern of making friendships that were bad for her. The typical pattern was that she would be adopted by an older girl, who would make her feel special. 'Attention' would then be followed by 'rejection'. It was painful for other people to see this happening, but more painful to realise that, no matter how clearly they could see what was happening, Mary could not seem to see it at all. Until one day she did ...

Thinking about it later she realised that for some time she had felt awful inside, and knew that something about the way she made friendships was quite wrong. Interestingly, even though she had received plenty of advice about the matter, at school and at home, she was none the wiser. She simply did not recognise herself as the girl being described. Until she did ...

Although miserable, she had been able to get involved in a local drama group. Over a period of a year it had become like a refuge to her. For the first time she had become used to taking up roles in the drama group (a nagging wife; a blind girl; a bully) that she could leave behind in the room as she walked out. Doing this week in and week out finally allowed her to realise that in 'real life' she was caught up in another role. As soon as she realised this, the quality of her friendships changed decisively. She was able to move away from the kind of intense short-term relationships that were causing her so much pain, and protect herself more by joining supportive groups as a basis for friendship.

Mary's story shows that it can be difficult to get into a position from which you can observe yourself. Sometimes it can seem as if we ourselves are the last to understand what is going on inside us.

> 'Sometimes it can seem as if we ourselves are the last to understand what is going on inside us.'

It is interesting that comments from those outside the situation did not help Mary to look at herself. It took the experience of feeling what it was like to be in different roles to enable her to look at herself in a new way. The ability to have an experience and – more importantly – to learn more about ourselves by thinking about it and feeling it is an important step in managing change.

SUMMARY

This chapter has looked at the types of change we experience, and how they can be managed, particularly during adolescence. Adolescence is a time of enormous change – physical, emotional, social – and we often feel overwhelmed, confused and unable to deal with it all. Some general rules, rather than a simple formula, can help us cope: to be adaptable, to use our minds and powers of observation, and be able to look inside ourselves, even though our feelings may be painful.

This is something that shouldn't be done alone. The next three chapters look at different aspects of the company you keep.

CHAPTER
TWO:

*THE COMPANY
YOU KEEP*:
FRIENDSHIPS
*Which
relationships are
good for you and
which are not?*

The next three chapters will try to answer the question we asked in the checklist given on page 2 of the Introduction:

❏ **Do you have positive relationships with those around you?**
What company do you keep? Do you have good friends? Are you able to hold on to a sense of your own individuality, or do you get lost in the crowd? Are you involved in a friendship that is not good for you? How do you relate to adults?

This chapter will look at the issues involved in making relationships, and the next chapter will concentrate on groups and gangs. After that, in Chapter 4, we will look at ways of building strong relationships with adults.

FRIENDSHIPS AND RELATIONSHIPS

Make a list of the main people you see during a typical week. List them in order of how much time you spend with them. Include family members in the list.

1	_____	**5**	_____
2	_____	**6**	_____
3	_____	**7**	_____
4	_____	**8**	_____

Now go through the list again and think about how much time you spend with each person, and how much you enjoy their company. There is space in the table below for you to record your thoughts. In the column marked 'What kind of company are they?' the words 'good' and 'not good' do not refer to the people themselves – they refer to the effect these people have on you: Do *you* feel good after spending time with them? Do they help you cope with life?

Name	What kind of company are they?			How often do you meet each week?		
	Good	Not good	Don't know	Once	2–5 times	Every day
1. _____						
2. _____						
3. _____						
4. _____						
5. _____						
6. _____						
7. _____						
8. _____						

Notice that the people you enjoy spending time with are not always the ones who you spend most time with. Where, for example, do you put brothers and sisters, if you have them? What do you think of the following illustration?

PETER'S STORY

Peter (14) was four years older than his brother Simon. There had been times when they had got on well together, mainly over games such as Pokemon trading, and in sport. In many ways they were very good companions for each other. But when he thought about it, Peter realised that enjoying Simon's company depended very much on finding something to do together – otherwise, they soon started to fight. The differences had become more obvious in the last 18 months or so. Peter thought that Simon was always trying to copy him and would never let him do anything on his own without wanting to try it too. Even when friends came round, Simon wanted to be there, and he seemed hurt when Peter wanted to be left on his own. Suddenly 11 seemed so much younger than 14. Peter really did not think that he felt close to Simon any more. He was troubled about it because they had been very close at one time, and, even now, when they had something to do together, it went well.

Peter's story shows that:

1. Relationships change, particularly sibling relationships.
2. The company we keep can include stressful relationships, but they may still be important.

> **For a closer look at this issue,**
> **see *Real Life Issues: Stress*, Chapter 3**

Now look back at your list of the people you see each week. How many of your relationships have changed recently? Which of them, for example, has become easier and which more difficult? Can you remember how things have changed over the last year? You may well be surprised to see that friendships do change over time, particularly during the teenage years. They change not only in terms of your

> *'... friendships ... change over time, ... not only in terms of your relationships with individuals but also in terms of the larger social groups that you become involved with.'*

relationships with individuals but also in terms of the larger social groups that you become involved with. Let's look at some different relationships before thinking about the issue of coping as it is applied to friendships and relationships. (Relationships with adults will be looked at in Chapter 4.)

Close friends

Part of your list may include time spent with a 'best friend'. However it happens, you may find that you and this friend seem to think the same way about life: the good things, sorrows, hurts and pains; and above all, the strong feelings it causes. Close friendships can take many forms: boy-boy; girl-girl; girl-boy. It can be very helpful to find someone you can talk to, particularly if it is not so easy to do this at school or in the family. It can be surprising to realise how important a close friend is to you and it is easy to get confused about the feelings that can arise from this, and wonder what they might mean.

Stephanie's story may help you think about deep friendships, and about how much we can be helped by them, even though they can be painful.

STEPHANIE'S STORY
Stephanie had always been good at making friends. She had also been quite good at falling out with them, getting together again, and moving on from time to time. However, she was very generous in

friendships – able to put herself into them with gusto. At 15 she became inseparable from Lucie and quite quickly they were meeting more at school, doing similar courses and seeing lots of each other after school and at weekends. Inevitably, this meant that Stephanie did less with her other friends, and she seemed to move away from a close relationship with her mother at more or less the same time.

Then Lucie gave her the bad news – her mother had been diagnosed with a serious illness, and because of this, the family would be moving to another part of the country, so Lucie would be doing A levels there. Stephanie was devastated. Seemingly for the first time she realised just how much of her life was arranged around her friendship with Lucie. After the move she did what she could to keep in touch: emails; long phone calls; even letters (though she found it difficult to write things down). Eventually she realised that life had moved on, the feelings died down, and she gradually made new friendships. However, she held on to the memory of the intense feelings she had been caught up in at that time. She remembered feeling that life itself had become pointless and terribly empty.

Later, when things became less intense, it occurred to her that the feelings she had experienced were very like an incident when she was very young and had lost her mother whilst out shopping. She remembered being absolutely terrified.

Stephanie's story shows that close friends can be a way of exploring troublesome relationships elsewhere in our lives. Stephanie's friendship with Lucie gathered to itself many feelings from elsewhere. It seems possible that the intensity of the friendship was connected with the difficult time she was having with her mother. Stephanie had always been close to her mother, sometimes rather clingy. It is interesting that one side-effect of the deep friendship with Lucie was

> *'... close friends can be a way of exploring troublesome relationships elsewhere in our lives.'*

that some of the dependency on her mother was also given up. By the time she had emerged from what had happened with Lucie, she had also established a different relationship with her mother. There was a more restrained, more 'adult' contact between them. At times Stephanie felt sad about this, but overall it seemed for the best.

Do you have any 'complicated' friendships like this at the moment?

Other friends

Not every friendship has to be at a 'best friend' level, nor does it have to last forever. It is quite normal for two people to be close for a while, and then move apart, whilst remaining acquaintances. You don't have to 'fall out' for this to happen, though that depends on the characteristics of the people involved. Sometimes, people want a neat solution to friendships, wanting to know who is 'in' or 'out', and they are not so comfortable with a kind of halfway house.

SOME RULES ABOUT FRIENDSHIP

At this point it might be a good idea to consider some rules about friendship.

Fulfilling a need

It is clear from Stephanie's experience (see above) that a major function of friendship is finding someone who can allow you to think, feel and talk about issues that would otherwise go round and round inside your head – or maybe not even get as far as your head!

Sometimes it is possible to make a friend and also do some sorting out about something else at the same time. Stephanie, for example, transferred some of her relationship with her mother to her friend Lucie. This seems to have been important for her: it made it possible to look at her developing relationship with her mother and help her to separate a little. This was important both for her mother and herself.

What about Lucie, though? What did she get out of it? Was she being 'used' by Stephanie? It was time for Stephanie to look at some aspects of her relationships with her own mother, but was it right that she should do this through Lucie? Wasn't this just 'using' Lucie – just taking advantage of her to work through some issues of her own? Surely this is not the basis for a real friendship at all?

These are important questions and they are also very difficult to answer! We do not know Lucie's view of the issue and whether or not she felt used by Stephanie; but it does not seem as if she did. In fact, it seemed that she also needed a friend at that time. We might say that friendship often involves an amount of self-interest. Nevertheless, there is a balance to be aimed at, where both people benefit.

'… there is a balance to be aimed at, where both people benefit.'

Respect for others

You may remember Mary's situation (see page 19). She became involved in a number of situations in which she was used by someone else. In order to change her relationships she had to get a view 'from the outside' of what was happening to her. Now there is no doubt that we can get into relationships that are, at best, unhelpful and at worst very harmful to us.

Why not make a short list, as honestly as you can, of those relationships in your life that are helpful, and those that are unhelpful?

But how does it happen? How do we make bad choices, or set out to use relationships selfishly for our own ends? Is it just chance and sheer bad luck? It is not usually either. The friendships and relationships we make are very much connected with the view we have of ourselves.

Sometimes (not always) our relationships are connected with difficult areas of ourselves, particularly those we do not like to think about. If, for example, we have a view of ourselves as victims being picked on all the time, it is not surprising that we might want to escape that view of ourselves, and want to be able to say to someone, 'Why not pick on someone else for a change?'

But remember, there *are* good friendships. Lasting friendships are usually built on a positive image of ourselves: a view where we feel we can cope with our own faults and problems and where we are able to tolerate those of others.

> **For a closer look at some of the issues covered in this chapter, see *Real Life Issues: Sex & Relationships* and *Real Life Issues: Bullying***

SUMMARY

This chapter has looked at friendships of different kinds, and shown how the deepest friendships are usually built on mutual respect. But so far we have only looked at separate friendships with other individuals – what about the larger friendship groups that we become part of? This is what we will look at in the next chapter.

CHAPTER THREE

THE COMPANY YOU KEEP: GROUPS AND GANGS

How to be yourself in the company of others

The checklist in the Introduction to this book asks an important question about what company you keep:

❏ Are you able to hold on to a sense of your own individuality, or do you get lost in the crowd?

This chapter will look at 'the crowd' – ie groups and gangs. Sometimes these two words are used as if they are the same. This chapter defines

FACT BOX

Individuality: having a distinct identity – your own particular interests, personality and opinions, and a sense of yourself as unique and separate from those around you.

groups as being able to help us to hold on to and even develop our individuality, and **gangs** as causing us to lose a sense of ourselves. A group is a collection of individuals who just happen to like each other's company, but in a gang individuality tends to get overtaken by the needs of the stronger members of the gang.

GROUP OR GANG? THE CHOICE

There is a famous example of group versus gang in the book *Lord of the Flies* by William Golding.

The book looks at what might happen if a group of children and adolescents were shipwrecked on an island without knowing how soon – if ever – they would be rescued.

At first they are a group of frightened children, but on the whole they trust their leader, Ralph. He is able to unite them through inspired leadership and he organises them around their two principal tasks as a group:

■ Keep alive the hope of rescue by lighting and maintaining the beacon
■ Keep the group alive until they are rescued by finding food, shelter, etc.

Gradually Jack, who was defeated in the election for leader, starts to undermine Ralph and the group starts to break up. Individuals have a difficult choice to make. Should they stick with Ralph, who is keeping his mind on the main task of being rescued by the adults, or should they join Jack? Jack is in charge of finding food and hunting, and it is easy to see why joining him is appealing. Soon most of them are gathered round Jack and on the other 'side' there is only Ralph and a boy they call Piggy.

Bit by bit, Jack becomes bolder and more assertive in his leadership. Some of the boys who joined him realise too late that they have given up their freedom in return for being fed. As long as they do what they are told there will be no trouble but they have no *choice* over what they do. Others, however, are filled with excitement at being part of this powerful organisation, or gang, and delighted to feel its strength as they raid the camp of Ralph and Piggy. Eventually tragedy strikes and Piggy is killed before the adults finally arrive on the scene.

> *'As long as they do what they are told there will be no trouble but they have no* choice *over what they do.'*

It's pretty rare to end up shipwrecked on a desert island, having to plan how to survive and how to get rescued, so the story might seem a little far-fetched. But the story's really about groups and gangs. Let's have a look at groups first.

GROUPS

Everyone knows in some way what a group is – it's obvious and very easy to describe from the outside. It is a different matter to tell someone what it feels like to be in a group. People join groups for different reasons, and everyone's experience is different. One reason why people join groups is simply for company and the opportunity to do things together.

Joining a group is rarely part of a deliberate plan – very few people say to themselves 'today I'm going to join a group'. It does not happen like that. Instead, people are drawn together for all kinds of reasons. When you look at it from the outside it can be interesting to see how people take up different roles. For example, a group might include:

- Ruth (the very thin one)
- Sylvia (the talkative one)
- Tom (the lazy one)
- Donna (in her own world).

At times it might seem that the group has developed a collective identity, which includes different elements and characteristics from each individual member, all merged together to form a larger 'group' identity, which is affected by the welfare of all its members. Different members of the group are reminded of different parts of themselves in this way. So, for example, someone who is normally very quiet can be helped to think about *why* they are so quiet by a very active and talkative member of the group. Or when Ruth talks about being very thin and maybe about having difficulties with food, other members of the group are able to consider their attitude to food too.

> **For a closer look at anorexia and other eating disorders, see *Real Life Issues: Eating Disorders***

Being in a group is a way of being able to pour out your feelings to others, and also of taking in their feelings. You are supporting others, but also making it easier to discuss things about yourself that, on your own, it would be difficult to think about.

What about individuality?

You may join a group for particular reasons – which may not even be clear to you at the time – but then find that you no longer feel the same way that you did at the beginning. To use the example given above, the group may not want 'Tom the lazy one' to become 'Tom the very busy and active one'. They may well want him to be the one they had become accustomed to and needed in a particular role. So for example, if Tom suddenly started working extremely hard, other members of the group might start to feel worried that they weren't doing enough work themselves.

In most groups, as they develop, there will always be a struggle between what the group needs and what the individual needs. Just take a moment to look at a group you are involved in, and think about how it has changed. Membership of a group (or groups) is a very important way of coping with changes in your life. But what characteristics must a group have in order to grow and to be a positive experience for its members?

> *'Membership of a group (or groups) is a very important way of coping with changes in your life.'*

1. You need not start behaving differently or strangely to join it. It can accept you as you are.
2. You can talk freely and also change your mind.
3. You are wanted for who you are.
4. The group can accept ideas and change direction.
5. Although you might be given a role and a name within the group, you can change it if you want to.

TIP BOX

Some groups are more flexible and democratic than others, but the important thing is to be able to take part in the group without feeling that you have to get rid of your own personality.

GANGS

In a gang, you don't have the freedom to be yourself or to change how the gang operates. The following case study shows how gang membership can appeal, and how it can get out of control.

A GANG MEMBER'S STORY

A former gang member recently described his time in a gang. He did not refer to his membership as 'gang membership', but talked instead about 'linking up with one or two others'. They began to steal – petty theft at first and then robbery with violence. Drugs followed, both using and selling, and more people joined the gang. He felt a sense of strength and power as they walked the streets together. For him, this was the main thrill.

One day, however, he saw things in a different light. He realised that his whole life was about being a gang member: fights, drugs, robbery, etc. There was no room for anything else; no future plans outside this. He was shocked to discover that this had happened – that he had become callous and unfeeling about the people he beat up and stole from. Eventually he managed to leave the gang and his old way of life, and probably the first step in making the break was looking at himself and confronting what he saw in the 'mirror'.

Not all gangs are violent in this way! But they share this tendency to ignore the individual gang members and get carried away, losing touch with the real people whose lives they may affect – both within and outside the gang. Despite this, however, gang membership can seem very appealing.

Why are gangs attractive?
THE POSITIVE SIDE

There is strength in numbers. This is shown very clearly in *Lord of the Flies*: even though they may not have liked Jack, the children did like his good leadership and the feeling it gave them to be part of a strong gang. They could rampage through the island without feeling afraid, and put aside their fear that they would never be rescued.

So belonging to a large group and feeling stronger as a result is certainly one very powerful reason for belonging to a gang. It can also seem to fill a gap in one's life. A recent survey suggests that teenagers generally spend almost 70% (ie 16 hours 48 minutes per day) of their time alone. Even if you spend ten hours a day asleep, this still leaves you with six waking hours alone. Of course this is only an average, and so for some people the figure is higher, and for some it's lower. But it's still a long time to be alone with a TV screen, MP3 player or your own thoughts. No wonder the thought of being in a group or gang is appealing. Sometimes it's a case of 'beggars can't be choosers', at least some of the time. We may not approve of all that goes on in the group, but it's better than being terribly alone.

THE NEGATIVE SIDE

This depends on the kind of group or gang you are in, but the main issue is that you can lose control and cease to have much say in what is happening. Sometimes a gang is involved in activities that most – or at least some – of its members don't want to play any part in, but they feel they have to participate or they'll be looked down on or even thrown out of the gang. The peer pressure in a gang can be very strong. One example is a recent series of attacks by a gang on passengers on a tube train in London. People on the train reported how difficult it was to appeal to the individuality of the youths in the gang as they robbed the passengers.

Let's think about the members of the gang. How did they get into it? Did they really want to be there? Were they all 'leaders'? One eyewitness talked of looking into blank eyes, not able to get through to the person behind them. It seems clear that in order to get into that kind of gang and, above all, to stay in it, you have to do something to your mind – to the way you see other people. Above all, the cost is losing sensitivity and building a hard shell between yourself and others. But does this matter?

> *'… the cost is losing sensitivity and building a hard shell between yourself and others.'*

Try doing this experiment with a friend. Make up a scene where you come across someone younger than you. You bully them and demand money. Now reverse roles. You might be quite surprised at the powerful feelings that are experienced. Try to describe the feelings, because in fact they are yours. It can be quite a shock to come across different, apparently opposite, versions of ourselves. We all have it in us to be the bully or to be bullied, to be the thinking member of a group or the switched-off, insensitive gang member.

> **For a closer look at bullying, see**
> ***Real Life Issues: Bullying***

WHY BELONGING TO A GROUP IS IMPORTANT

Although groups can sometimes turn into gangs, they are certainly not 'bad news'. Belonging to a supportive group can help us cope with life, as the case study below shows.

MARIA'S STORY

Maria found the change from junior school to secondary school very difficult indeed. She felt very lonely and taken aback by the large groups, the larger number of teachers, and the roughness of fellow pupils, particularly boys, with whom she had never got on (they reminded her of her brother, with whom she was always fighting). This changed over the next three years.

At first she linked up with girls who were a bit like herself. In a seemingly quiet way they began to support each other, particularly in school, where each of them would have found it difficult to manage alone. They were even able to acknowledge differences between them and bring others into the group. Looking back, three years later, Maria was amazed at the difference between the timid person she had been aged 12 and how she felt at 15, when she was busily going through her diary trying to find a space for school work between social engagements. The original group had survived but was unrecognisable from the tightly organised 'survival unit' of the early days. There were boys now, and a number of floating members who seemed to appear for different reasons and then move away again. Maria herself was a case in point. She had a special attachment to the original group who had helped her so much, but she also went around with others. Sometimes these different groups overlapped, but she also now rather liked the fact that she could go between different groups, and could have a bit of a rest from the others. What a difference a few years make! Maria could not see how she could have coped without group membership.

Maria's focus overall was on groups. But what about the floating members, who seemed to appear for different reasons before moving on? Is it possible that their motivation was different from that of Maria, even though they appeared in the same place as her? Denise and

Amy were 'floating members' of a group – the case study below shows what they gained from their temporary group membership.

DENISE AND AMY'S STORIES

Denise and Amy were members of a large Friday night youth club. They joined it at a time when they were quite timid about social groups. They used to attend in order to get the gossip, and to find out what was 'in' and what was 'out'. For them the loose (too loose they felt, looking back on it) structure enabled them to go along without having to get to know the others. They wanted to remain unknown but have a good look at what went on.

> **For a closer look at some of these issues, see *Real Life Issues: Sex & Relationships***

SUMMARY

This chapter has looked at individuality. It has shown how we need to hold on to our own sense of who we are and what we do, and to choose to belong to groups that we find fulfilling and supportive. We need to make sure we don't get trapped inside something unhelpful.

'…we need to hold on to our own sense of who we are and what we do, and to choose to belong to groups that we find fulfilling and supportive.'

We've looked at membership of groups and gangs and the different reasons why you might choose one over another. It might be helpful to summarise some characteristics of both.

Group	Gang
Individuality retained	Individuality given up in return for security
Character of group is made rich through individual membership	Strong leadership
Members work effectively and creatively	Strongly defined direction

EXERCISE

Choose one situation that you are involved with personally. List its characteristics. Try to categorise it in terms of 'group' or 'gang' membership.

So far we have looked at friendships and friendship groups with people of a similar age. The next chapter will deal with family life and look at ways of building strong relationships with adults.

CHAPTER FOUR:

THE COMPANY YOU KEEP: RELATING TO ADULTS
Seeing each other's viewpoint

On the whole, adolescents find it difficult to relate to adults and the opposite is certainly also true. The word **relate** is here because it is important to think of two points of view. This chapter will look at some of the difficult areas and suggest ways of setting up better communication.

FAMILY LIFE

Life in families never stands still. It is important not to underestimate the power of external events such as:

- Moving house – to a smaller or larger place, or to a different part of the country
- Birth of a brother or sister
- Death of a relation or close member of the family, such as a parent, brother or sister
- Divorce, the re-organisation of home life and the need to relate to two parents in two different settings
- Change in employment, leading to a difference in income.

It is easy to see that any of these events would affect family life – but exactly how would it do so, and what qualities do we need to help us cope? Let's refer back to the checklist in the Introduction:

❑ **Are you adaptable?**

Do you manage to think about new situations and adopt a flexible approach, or do you find it difficult to change your mind? Do you get caught up in routines that can't be changed?

❑ **Are you resilient?**

What happens to you when something goes badly? Do you give up, or can you bounce back?

It is the first time that we have put adaptability and resilience together. Difficult change is unwelcome, and it is not easy to know what kind of impact an external event will have. Consider an event which may have happened to you, like moving house. In the table below, some of the changes it causes have been listed, along with a grid to record how much they may have affected you and your family (1 indicates the smallest effect; 5 indicates the largest effect). For each change, circle the number that best reflects the impact you and your family have felt.

Impact

It is difficult to know what impact any change will have. Sometimes the smallest things can have a very big effect on us – and different people can react in different ways. The reason why moving can be difficult is that in some strange way a part of you seems to get left behind in the move. It is as if the house you left was not a house, but a bundle of memories: some painful, some funny, others worrying; but all part of you.

There are many more serious changes in the list on page 41, including birth and death, which everyone recognises as big events. (For example, we looked at Jane's story in the Introduction. She was only

Event	Changes	Impact on you					Impact on your family				
Moving house to another part of the country	New school	1	2	3	4	5	1	2	3	4	5
	Loss of friends	1	2	3	4	5	1	2	3	4	5
	Anxiety about making new friends	1	2	3	4	5	1	2	3	4	5
	New room	1	2	3	4	5	1	2	3	4	5
	Packing and unpacking	1	2	3	4	5	1	2	3	4	5
	Loss of favourite places	1	2	3	4	5	1	2	3	4	5
	Loss of routines	1	2	3	4	5	1	2	3	4	5
	Different transport	1	2	3	4	5	1	2	3	4	5
Total											

16 when her father died after a long illness.) You can make your own version of the table above and fill it in with the changes caused by a major event in your own life.

You will notice that the 'impact' column is not only for you but also for members of your family. Are you able to fill this in, or don't you know how they feel? It is surprising how differently members of the same

'It is surprising how differently members of the same family can feel about something that has happened, and how difficult it can be to talk about this.'

family can feel about something that has happened, and how difficult it can be to talk about this.

HOW TO INTERPRET YOUR SCORE

Once you have filled in all the columns, add up your total and your family's total. A low score for you and/or your family indicates that you are good at coping with things and moving on – it is likely that you are both adaptable and resilient. If your score is higher, this suggests that you are good at holding onto things. We can be upset by change of all kinds. Even though we may move on to other friendships, relationships or places to live, it is possible for our minds to remain 'stuck' in the old situation. It sometimes seems like part of us can get left behind and we are scared of losing touch with precious memories. At some point it is important to allow memories and feelings to 'make the trip' from the old situation to the new one. The process involves mourning, facing up to the fact that something has gone, and making an evaluation of it. The point is that families try to hold on to their history without being aware of this in a conscious way. This makes it difficult to accept change.

ADOLESCENCE

As we saw in Chapter 1, adolescence is about change, and so it is not surprising that you will have clashes with your family, and that they will disagree with you. The process of adolescence makes everyone think, adults and teenagers alike.

Clashes

Clashes and arguments often occur within the family over one or more of the points below. (They have been presented in the same way as your family might present them to you!)

■ Appearance – clothes too scruffy or too skimpy, hair too long or too short, needs washing, not tidy enough

> 'The changing nature of the family is central. Teenagers are affected by instability of family life which causes a lot of difficulty; it muddles up roles and there is not the support for young people as previously.'
>
> **John Coleman, Director, Trust for the Study of Adolescence**

- Homework – too short (rarely too long), not done
- Telephone – too long (rarely too short), needs paying for
- Going out – always too long.

These might sound light-hearted, but let's not underestimate the difficulty for families of these flashpoints. They can have a major impact on life, making for a very unpleasant time.

Is there a way of understanding them? The following example might help:

MIRANDA'S STORY

Miranda is 13. She says: 'I am really fed up at the moment. I know Mum's upset about Dad leaving but she won't leave me alone. She needs to know where I am all the time. It's not really worth the fight I have to have when I want to go out. If I go somewhere I just know that she will ring at some point to check that I am really there. It is upsetting to think she doesn't trust me. It gets worse: she has started introducing bedtimes, saying that I am a growing girl and need my beauty sleep! I don't know how much longer I can put up with it. I could just kill my Dad for getting me into this.'

Miranda's mother, as a response to the shock of her partner leaving, has started to treat Miranda as if she was a younger version of herself. A baby, in fact. It is as if the shock of losing one person has made her determined not to lose another, and what better way than to hold her tight like the baby she used to be, rather than allow her to be an adolescent heading towards adulthood, and likely to leave home soon? Miranda understands that her mother is behaving out of character and is trying not to react too fiercely, but it does not seem possible that she will be able to put up with this situation for very long.

Living in the past

Even when there is no particular stress, such as divorce, it can be difficult to be freed from the story of who you were when you were younger. You can probably remember countless stories (and pictures) of what you used to be like, brought out amid scenes of merriment at family gatherings. It can sometimes feel as if the new person, the you who is growing in all directions, is not wanted.

> 'Even when there is no particular stress … it can be difficult to be freed from the story of who you were when you were younger.'

LYDIA'S STORY

Lydia describes how adolescence affected her relationship with her daughter, Karen: 'At 14 Karen started to develop a figure. She looked really wonderful and I was proud of her, and amazed at how confident she was about making friends. I remember being painfully shy at her age, and I certainly wasn't allowed to go out as she is … She has changed so quickly over the last year that I haven't got used to it. I keep thinking back to when she was younger, and I know that

she is not as confident as she seems. I am trying to get better at
giving her more independence but it is not easy.'

Karen's mother Lydia has been taken aback by the pace of change,
and finds herself falling back on earlier memories. But what about you,
an adolescent yourself? Do you fall back on the past too? At first sight
this might seem unlikely. After all, the main cause of arguments so far
has been the difficulty you feel when your parents will not realise that
you are growing up and need to be treated as a person with more
maturity than before. Derek, a father aged 42, did feel that part of the
difficulty of being a parent to a teenage son was that he was always
being compared to an earlier form of himself. In the case study below,
he talks about how he thinks his son Darren thinks of him:

DEREK'S STORY

'I felt that I could not keep up with Darren as he became a teenager
and better at sport. I felt he wanted me to be able to play with him
as I had done when he was much younger. It was difficult for him to
accept that I am a middle-aged father and not as fit as I was and he
certainly can't accept this. I don't think he has let me grow older in his
mind, and he feels that I am not interested in him anymore, and that
is certainly not true.'

This suggests that Darren was holding onto a memory that his father
felt was very resistant to change. This is different from the typical
example of pictures being taken out at family gatherings: Darren
obviously wasn't around when his father was 14! Nevertheless, he
seems to have filed away a picture of energy and sports activity that
had had its day. His father felt that this got in the way of Darren
recognising the new ways in which their relationship could develop.
Food for thought!

> **For a closer look at family relationships, see**
> ***Real Life Issues: Sex & Relationships***

Responsibility

It is possible for families, parents and teenagers to live too much in
the past, without realising it. This makes it difficult to adapt to change,
which moves on regardless. An important theme running through the
examples above is responsibility. The tension within families, and
between teenagers and individual parents, is often connected with the
issue of how much responsibility can be taken by teenagers, or held
back by parents.

What is 'taking responsibility', and why is it so important? It is
connected with the following:

1. Being adaptable, being able to make a judgement based on the
   situation you are really being faced with, and not on the one you
   would like.
2. Knowing about the company you are in.
3. Using your mind and being prepared to change it.
4. Being in touch with your feelings, and having a good sense of
   whether a situation is good for you or not.

It will come as no surprise that these are some of the general
principles of coping that were described in the Introduction. If you
have qualities matching the list above then you are likely to be able to
cope with problems in a controlled and responsible way.

SUMMARY

You will notice that in this chapter we have left out phrases like 'It's my
life, I can do what I want' and 'You're only a child' because these are

more to do with avoiding the real issue between teenagers and adults. The real issue is to do with taking responsibility and developing the adaptability and resilience that can help us get through a lot of the changes in life that might at first seem daunting.

> *'The real issue is to do with taking responsibility and developing the adaptability and resilience that can help us get through a lot of the changes in life…'*

Another quality which can help us cope is self-regard. We will look at this in more detail in the next chapter.

CHAPTER FIVE:

SELF-REGARD
How to look after yourself

In the Introduction we asked:

❑ **Do you have self-regard?**

Are you in touch with your personal history? Are you kind in the way you think about yourself? Or are you very self-critical – too harsh with yourself?

In order to answer these questions this chapter will be asking:

◼ How do we ask questions of identity?
◼ How do we come to know ourselves?

THE DIFFICULTY WITH ASKING QUESTIONS OF IDENTITY

Some questions are far more difficult than others, as you will see from the following list:

1. What is your favourite colour?
2. Who is your favourite singer?

3 Can you describe the main strengths and weaknesses of your best friend?

4 Who are you?

Answering the first three questions might be quite difficult. Question 1 might be a little tricky as you may not have given much thought to colours. Question 2 might cause some discussion since your tastes change over time, and you may have more than one 'favourite'. You'll probably be able to say quite a lot about your best friend once you put your mind to it, even though you may find it hard to make a start. But what about the last question: 'Who are you?' How is it possible to start answering a question like this?

One way to make a start might be to put down the questions and issues you find important at the moment. The case studies below show how a seemingly small thing like how we feel about our clothes or our friends can be part of our search to discover and express who we are.

MIKE'S STORY

Mike went from being easy-going and not caring too much about the clothes he wore to being very 'picky'. His clothes now seemed all wrong. He wasn't sure how he wanted to look but he knew that he had to change. What seemed to matter most was the fact that what he currently had should be scrutinised and thrown out if it seemed too dated or too young. Previously he had chosen clothes with his parents, but now it seemed important to make his own shopping trips and his own choices (though he was still dependent on his parents for money to do so).

WHAT MIKE'S STORY SHOWS

Mike regards the clothes issue as the most important question about identity at the moment. There is clearly an important search going on behind the question about what to wear. His 'pickiness' about his clothes is a way of taking responsibility for himself and of looking closely at anything that was connected with him at an earlier age. It's not only a way of leaving behind something belonging to the past, but also of re-defining his personal space.

Attitudes to identity change from time to time, like part of a bigger puzzle that needs to be looked at bit by bit. Sometimes the question of clothes becomes very complicated and mixed up with other issues.

SAMANTHA'S STORY
Samantha started to feel very strange about her best friend Caitlin. She noticed that whenever she bought new clothes it was only a matter of time before Caitlin wore something very similar. It wasn't just clothes either, but homework, hobbies and even sport. It became difficult to mention anything without feeling that it would soon be taken over. The problem for Samantha was that she liked Caitlin, but did not like the feeling of having her own attempts to work out what she liked being taken over from her.

The search for identity can become attached to a number of different questions and preoccupations. At any one time it can seem that these are the real issues of identity rather than the underlying themes.

EXERCISE
What constitutes your identity issues at the moment? Make a list of things that are important to you – it could include your interests, hobbies, friends, concerns, ambitions...

How did you get on? How long is your list? The trouble with the question of identity is that the more possible answers we come up with and the longer the list we make, the more confused we get.

> *'The trouble with the question of identity is that the more possible answers we come up with and the longer the list we make, the more confused we get.'*

These thoughts come from inside us and they never seem to stop. They can range from 'What clothes should I wear?' or 'What groups should I hang out with?' to 'Why have these spots appeared on my face?' or 'How can I possibly go out with a face looking like this?'

HARRY'S STORY

Harry started to sleep badly, and eventually talked to his mother. His mind seemed to be constantly full of 'useless' questions: What will I be? Why aren't I good at sport? Why can't I keep friends? Am I gay? Many questions on all sorts of topics would flood his mind, and it seemed as if he had no control over them. If he didn't know better he would have thought they had been planted inside him by someone else. They could not possibly come from him, could they? Wherever they came from he didn't want them. How could he get rid of them?

In fact, Harry was able to talk to someone about the questions and gradually they died down. But what are these questions? How do we control them? How do we decide whether or not they are helpful? Read on…

HAVING A SENSE OF PERSONAL HISTORY

When there are lots of questions buzzing around in your head at the same time it's difficult to think properly about who you are. They can seem overwhelming – you might start to panic about how you can

> *'You have been around for quite a long time and you may find that you know much more about yourself than you think.'*

ever answer them all. But wait a minute! Aren't you forgetting something? You have been around for quite a long time and you may find that you know much more about yourself than you think.

Personal history does not mean a memory of actual events in your life. It means gradually building up a sense of knowing yourself deep down, based on all the things you have done. Unfortunately, the sense of knowing ourselves can seem to vanish when we panic or are going through a crisis of confidence about ourselves. But there are ways to develop this kind of self-awareness and sense of personal history.

Becoming aware of yourself

Find the time to be by yourself for a few minutes whenever you can. Gradually become more aware of the thoughts you are having. Become aware of them, and then gently move them away. Try to become more aware of what feelings you are having. Are you happy? Are you sad? Are you jealous? Are you really angry but can't show it? Become aware of these feelings and try to move on.

Try to get to a point where you are not following a particular line of thought in a logical way, but remain focused on yourself. You will be surprised at the kinds of thoughts that come to mind. You may remember dreams, or a completely new thought about yourself may occur to you. When a thought of this kind arrives, it is a good idea to write it down or remember it. Gradually you will gather quite a number of these thoughts 'from within' and be able to distinguish them from the other unwelcome thoughts that come into your mind as surface anxieties.

SELF-REGARD

It is helpful to know our style, our way of relating to ourselves. When we talk about relating, we're usually talking about relating to someone else. But how we think about and relate to others is connected with how we relate to ourselves. Try the following quiz to find out how you look at yourself.

'... how we think about and relate to others is connected with how we relate to ourselves.'

SELF-REGARD QUESTIONNAIRE

Indicate whether you strongly disagree, disagree, are neutral, agree or strongly agree with the statements below by ticking the appropriate box. When you have finished, add up your score and see what it shows about your self-regard. Just remember there are no right or wrong answers and the questions are not meant to trick you!

	Strongly disagree (1 point)	Disagree (2 points)	Neutral (3 points)	Agree (4 points)	Strongly agree (5 points)
I always think I could have done better.	1	2	3	4	5
I compare myself unfavourably to my friends.	1	2	3	4	5
I frequently tell myself off in my mind.	1	2	3	4	5
I think I need to punish myself for doing things badly.	1	2	3	4	5

	Strongly disagree (1 point)	Disagree (2 points)	Neutral (3 points)	Agree (4 points)	Strongly agree (5 points)
I turn against others when things go badly for me.	1	2	3	4	5
I can't get any rest from a critical voice inside myself.	1	2	3	4	5
I am not able to give myself praise when I do well.	1	2	3	4	5
It does not help me to think of an approving voice when I am trying hard.	1	2	3	4	5

HOW TO INTERPRET YOUR SCORE

The purpose of the quiz is to find out about different ways of looking at yourself, rather than to point you to a particular suggestion or course of action.

■ **A high score (30–40)** shows that you tend to criticise yourself a lot – perhaps you often accuse yourself of failing. Sometimes it can seem as if the only way to get the best out of yourself is to be unkind, and push yourself to the limit.

■ **A medium score (18–29):** If your total score is made up of neutral scores, you may not really be aware of what you feel about some of these issues. Perhaps it would be helpful to find some time alone to think about them (see the exercise described above). If your total is made up of a combination of high and low scores, then try to look for a pattern. A pattern of alternating scores suggests a very lively exchange of views going on inside your head!

■ **A low score (8–17)** points to a positive outlook that might be rather self-congratulatory. Are you able to be self-critical?

WHAT TO DO ABOUT YOUR SCORE

The most important purpose of the exercise above is to provide information. It is helpful to know how we influence situations and what our starting point is. It is very difficult for us ever to look at ourselves in a completely detached, objective way – but if we can recognise that we are biased when we think about ourselves, this can be very helpful. For example, if you know that you can be hard on yourself then this knowledge can be helpful in moderating your approach. It is important to know that each of us has our own way of influencing conversations and interactions.

It is far better to think of your approach to yourself in terms of 'difference', rather than in terms of right or wrong: everyone has a unique, individual way of relating to themselves – although having to put up with an internal voice at one of the extremes (constantly condemning, constantly congratulating, or being entirely judgement-free) can make life very difficult in different ways.

> **For a closer look at how you relate to yourself, see *Real Life Issues: Confidence & Self-Esteem***

SUMMARY

In this chapter we have seen how difficult, and how important, it is to establish a sense of your own identity and to recognise your own particular ways of relating to yourself. Part of this process involves asking yourself difficult questions and being prepared to spend time thinking things through deeply. This can sometimes seem very stressful and some people find ways of avoiding the issue. We will look at this in more detail in the next chapter.

CHAPTER SIX:

CRUTCHES
Habits: a help or a hindrance?

In the Introduction we asked:

❏ **Can you get by without needing emotional 'crutches'?**
Are you able to manage day by day, or do you need drugs (eg alcohol, cigarettes, illegal drugs) to help you get through?

This chapter will look at:

▨ Why we need emotional 'crutches'
▨ The way we use things – positive and negative
▨ Whether objects and habits are friends or foes.

WHY 'CRUTCHES'?

The word 'crutches' can be used to describe a lot of things that help us to cope with life. Sometimes we hardly notice ourselves using them, whilst at other times they become permanent companions, whether we like it or not. An important guiding rule in this chapter will be: can you let your own feelings come to the surface, to be aware of them and express them when appropriate? Or do you get embarrassed, push feelings down or pretend they are not there?

FACT BOX

Crutch: a support for a lame person, usually with a crosspiece at the top fitting under the armpit; any support or prop.
(The Concise Oxford Dictionary)

THE WAY WE USE THINGS – POSITIVE AND NEGATIVE

Our interest in ourselves and our possessions goes back almost to the beginning of our lives. Have you ever closely observed a baby or toddler discovering that he or she can move and start to make an impression on the world outside? These can be magical moments. For a while, everything a baby discovers is given the 'mouth test' – the baby instinctively puts everything it grabs straight into its mouth. The lips are used in this way as they are a young child's most sensitive search mechanism. But is there something else going on, too? Maybe everything within reach is being given the 'Is it edible or not?' test. Or is the child leaving his or her mark on the thing – laying claim to it?

This last suggestion is an appealing theory because this process of taking things and marking them as uniquely our own continues throughout our lives. For example, your mother might pick up a particular cushion from the sofa while recounting the holiday when it was bought. Many teenagers still have their first teddy bears, battered toys that show every one of their 'pet years' in their fur. You may have

'… this process of taking things and marking them as uniquely our own continues throughout our lives.'

something similar. Why not write down your ten favourite possessions and the memory or memories that accompany them?

Task

It is not only 'things' we collect. Throughout our life we also develop routines and activities around which we structure our time. Try writing a list of your ten favourite routines or activities. The list below gives some ideas to get you started – you might be able to add to them:

- Shopping on a Saturday afternoon
- Meeting friends
- Playing in a group
- Playing in a team
- Being alone on the computer
- Downloading music onto an MP3 player
- Doing homework in front of the television.

What you might find surprising when you make your own list is just how much of our time is taken up with our routines. Here's an example from Fiona (aged 17).

I love Friday evenings! I get home, have a quick meal, change (into anything really) and set off to pick up Elaine. We go to Helen's house and she is never ready. Eventually all five of us have arrived and we go out for a drink somewhere. Sometimes we stay at someone's house, even sleep over if the weather is bad. We don't do much really, but we go back a long way and it is good to talk. I suppose we just like the routine!

Fiona (and the group) take comfort from being able to predict how their Friday evening will go. The details are not planned, but there is a predictability about the routine that is satisfying to them. It's as if they can relax and give themselves over to it.

Perhaps it all seems a little too predictable. Do all the members of the group really enjoy their Friday evening routine, or do they wish they could change in favour of something else? Groups that seem perfect for all their members do tend to come to a halt.

COMPANIONS OR TYRANTS

When do routines and habits stop being a pleasurable way of enjoying ourselves and start to make us feel that we are in the grip of something we can't control? In some ways this question is similar to the difference between groups and gangs discussed in Chapter 3.

The group knows its members' names, takes the trouble to think things through, and accepts ideas from all group members. A gang, on the other hand, has a feeling of anonymity about it, and it often acts as though there were no individual members, only a single tyrannical voice. This is similar to what can happen to routines: they can become tyrannical, demanding obedience and starting to take over your life. Of course, not everyone moves from a harmless social routine to a dangerous habit. Some people stay within a safe social scene, whilst others seem to drift into dangerous habits from the beginning.

'… routines … can become tyrannical, demanding obedience and starting to take over your life.'

PAUL'S STORY

Paul used to belong to a 'safe' group that partied together. There was some cannabis smoking, but in the context of the group as a whole. It seemed that the group held each other together. However, Paul got more and more determined to push the group into places it had never been. Inevitably the group became confused by this and Paul was put under pressure to conform with the group's activities. His answer was to leave them. He became more and more isolated and became a heavy user of cannabis, moving on to 'skunk' (a particularly strong form of cannabis). Eventually his days became turned upside down. He would sleep until 4 pm and was usually under the influence of drugs.

We're not looking primarily at drugs: the issue here is how we cope with life generally. Paul's story shows clearly how the routine his drug use had got him into was not good for him, and how it took over his life.

So, if habits like drug use can be dangerous, why do we develop them? What is the purpose of these 'crutches'? As Fiona's case study showed, habits can be reassuring and pleasant. But they can also be used as an escape to avoid facing real problems – and this is when they become tyrannical. Paul's case illustrates this.

PAUL'S STORY – WHAT HAPPENED NEXT

Paul was able to talk about his experience. Increasingly he had found himself moving away from the group. It seemed as if the others in the group had had a happier upbringing than him. Cannabis at first helped him to forget some very painful memories, but he became more and more isolated. He felt that he was not addicted to drugs but would find it difficult to give them up because then the feelings would return. Also, he had become very attached to the actual sweet taste of 'skunk'. It seemed to remind him of baby food, such was the flavour. It was this, he thought, that would be very difficult to give up.

**For a closer look at drugs,
see *Real Life Issues: Addictions***

SUMMARY

Issues concerning drugs are very widespread and you will probably have to make a decision about them at some time. In this chapter we have seen how problems with emotional 'crutches' like drug use can often be linked to avoiding difficult issues in life.

'... problems with emotional "crutches" like drug use can often be linked to avoiding difficult issues in life.'

If you are able to develop self-regard (see Chapter 5), hang on to your sense of individuality and build strong relationships with those around you (see Chapters 2–4) then this will help you avoid problems with damaging 'crutches' like drug use.

Being in touch with your feelings and using your mind to think things through are also powerful qualities which help you cope with life without needing to use emotional 'crutches'. These qualities are explored more in the next chapter.

TIP BOX

Although it is not always easy, it is important that individual responsibility based on your own understanding of what you need for yourself should form the basis for decision making.

CHAPTER SEVEN:

USING YOUR MIND AND YOUR FEELINGS
Coping through thinking and feeling

In the checklist on page 2 we asked the following questions:

❏ **Are you able to use your mind?**

Everyone has a mind, but thinking can sometimes be painful. Does your mind help you to think things through, or do you give up and stop thinking about situations?

This chapter will look at:

■ The kind of thinking that is linked to feelings. This can be painful, particularly when you are actually doing it, but it can lead to a feeling of real accomplishment and self-regard.

■ Critical thinking.

LIFE AT SCHOOL

Attending secondary school or college is an important part of developing your mind. Sometimes it can be difficult to deal with school itself – the size of it is overwhelming; or it can be hard to make friends; or the task of learning in a more demanding place can be testing.

FACT BOX

Attitudes to school and to life
Surveys of the developed world show that UK teenagers have one of the worst staying-on rates in post-16 education and are more likely than most to take drugs, binge drink and have under-age sex.

Teenagers today are seen as much more disruptive at school than teenagers of earlier generations. Many people are concerned about this at the moment, but it may be useful to think about why schools and school life may be more difficult now than in the past.

Think about the following list. You may be able to add to it:

- The size of secondary schools
- Following in a successful sibling's footsteps
- Forming and maintaining friendships
- The groups you will be with
- Developing regular study habits
- Working well for teachers you like and for those you dislike
- Coping with the rules and regulations of a large institution
- Coping with the pressure of working for public exams such as GCSE, as well as AS and A2
- Dealing with the stress of applying for college or university.

How what you learn at school helps you cope with life

The list could be much longer than this: there are so many pressures today, certainly more than for previous generations. But schools make it possible to train for life itself, as well as for the subjects you are studying! This may not be an official reason for being at school, but it is important.

> *'...schools make it possible to train for life itself, as well as for the subjects you are studying!'*

Often, the first task at school seems not to be about work, but to be about forming alliances and friendships that will be helpful for protection and development, before you are able to function on your own.

In Chapter 3 we gave the example of Maria, who found the change from junior school to secondary school very difficult. It took her three years to settle properly. It wasn't impossible for her to use her mind during this time, but her efforts to learn were being interfered with by her other concerns, primarily connected with belonging. Her story shows how difficulties in one area can have a knock-on effect on other areas.

Opting out

It is not easy to 'buckle down' at school. It depends a lot on your temperament, as well as the school you are at. Possible obstacles to learning come not only from the external environment, but also from inside ourselves. You may feel pressure (however well-meaning it is) from parents and teachers: parents want their children to get good jobs; schools have to get good results. The question constantly being asked by school, in all kinds of hidden ways, is: 'Do you, as an individual, want to develop your mind with a view to doing well in life?'

With this question goes 'What do you want to do with your life?', which links back to the basic question 'Who are you?' As we saw in Chapter 5, this can be a difficult question to answer, and some people would rather rebel than face up to it.

Critical thinking

One of the biggest changes that take place while we are adolescents is in our capacity to think in a different, more mature way. We can call this 'critical thinking'.

JENNIFER'S STORY

Jennifer had worked very hard and done well at GCSEs, largely a result, she felt, of being diligent about written coursework, a frantic period of revision, and a mind like blotting paper when she needed it. She found it difficult to decide which were her best subjects but, on the whole, they were those where she liked the teacher, particularly if they gave good revision notes! She decided that one of her AS level subject choices should be English. Jennifer was quite confident of being able to take her work in her stride, but soon found herself unable to write an essay (of which she had done many). The main area of difficulty was in the area of literary criticism. Although she had had the general principles of criticism explained to her, Jennifer found it difficult to think for herself and to give her own views about literature. Her first try was not good: she simply summarised the play they were reading, rather than giving her views on the central characters. She tried again, and this time gave very strong views about the characters, but was told that her views, whilst strong, did not relate to the text.

It was not until she learned how to develop opinions based on evidence that she began to do well. Jennifer had really only thought of her brain as a memory bank: now she was developing a different skill altogether. She really felt her 'mind' as she had never felt it before.

The ability to think 'critically' – independently and objectively – is a very important skill. It is linked with developing the self-regard we saw in Chapter 5.

Learning to think with feeling

The problems we have to face in life are not as simple as literary criticism. The main difference is that when we are thinking about our own life, feelings and emotions are always present.

'… when we are thinking about our own life, feelings and emotions are always present.'

In order to think clearly about something over which we feel deeply, we need to carry out three different activities:

1 Become aware of our feelings at the time, eg:

- sad
- happy
- tired
- anxious
- lonely
- grateful.

2 Become aware of the problem:

■ write down the problem with as much detail as possible
■ write down the ideal solution
■ what stands in the way of the solution?
■ what will change in your life as a consequence?

3 Know what our style of relating to ourselves is – eg are you too strict or too soft?

■ what thoughts bother us and get in the way of thinking something through clearly?
■ what encouraging thoughts come from within?

It does seem rather complicated. Feelings affect the way we focus on the problem, and attempts to focus on the problem lead to feelings. We are buffeted by negative thoughts, and bolstered by positive ones.

SUMMARY

In this chapter we have seen that using your mind to help you think things through and cope with them involves critical thinking skills, self-regard and the ability to feel your own feelings, not push them away. We have seen how school can help you develop some of these qualities, but also how it can force you to ask questions about your future ('What do I want to be?') which you may not want to face. The next chapter will look at ways of thinking about the future without panicking about who you are and what you might leave behind.

CHAPTER EIGHT:

AN EYE TO THE FUTURE
Future plans: a help or an escape from thinking?

This chapter will help you work out a way to move forward, suggesting ways of:

■ Having plans for the future
■ Managing the past
■ Letting go of adolescence.

PLANS FOR THE FUTURE

Try the following exercise to find out how clear your future plans are.

Exercise

Without thinking too much about it, write down the following:

1 What I would most like to do.
2 Five jobs done by my family and relations.
3 What I definitely don't want to do.
4 Lifestyle and values:

    (a) the three most important ingredients in my life in ten years' time

    (b) what values will be most important to me.

This exercise can be quite difficult. The following notes may help.

1. What I would most like to do.
You don't have to focus on a particular career, profession or job title –
you could think instead about different types of activity (like 'office work',
'working with people', 'working outdoors' and so on). Put down whatever
you think of, even if it seems far-fetched. Sometimes we can be quite
surprised by an idea that comes from deep down inside. It is important
to remember that we have had the idea and to review it from time to
time. As well as the main idea, you may have others. Put these down
too. They may be more practical.

2. Five jobs done by my family and relations.
It is useful to bear in mind what your relations are doing. You might
decide you don't want to do a certain job because you've seen the
negative effects on a relative. For example, Kevin Keegan, former
manager of the England football team, saw football as a way of
avoiding working in the coalmines, which his relations had done.

3. What I definitely don't want to do.
It is important to ask yourself what *you* want to do rather than what
you think others might want you to do! One way of working out what's
right for you is to analyse what would definitely not suit you.

4. Lifestyle and values.
What thoughts do you have about, for example, relationships, what
country you might live in, what pets or belongings you might have, etc?
What personal code of conduct will you try to live by?

You will probably find that you have done much more thinking about
what you want to be and do than you imagine.

MANAGING THE PRESENT

There is a rather dreadful story of an employer who wrote in a reference about someone: 'His wishbone is where his backbone ought to be!' Cruel it may be, but it does draw attention to an important truth about plans and dreams about the future. It is important to have them, but they are just plans; and if we want them to happen we need to work out how to make them into reality.

It is important to be cautious about future plans. Plans and ideas are important, but there is no reason why they can't be changed. In order to reach a better understanding of ourselves, we must be able to use the experiences in our real lives to learn about ourselves, then apply what we have learned to our future.

'Plans and ideas are important, but there is no reason why they can't be changed.'

The relationship between having plans and reaching a better understanding of ourselves can be illustrated in Amir's story.

AMIR'S STORY

Amir had volunteered to spend part of his 'gap year' with an organisation that carried out building projects in deprived areas abroad. He had not been away from home before, so he found it difficult to make the transition to a strange country, and to a group seemingly more accustomed to being part of these projects than he was. For a while he felt quite sorry for himself and regretted having agreed to come. Some members of the group were older than he was, and two were at university. One was studying architecture, the other electronics, and they seemed to be accepted very quickly as the driving force behind the project. At first Amir felt quite jealous of them and wondered how he would get involved. It dawned on him that as an only child he had had quite a sheltered life until now. At first he felt quite an outsider, too slow to join in conversations that were dominated by some forceful characters. Gradually, however, he began to feel included.

His contribution to the project was to dig ditches and carry out other tasks under supervision. As time went on he became incredibly proud of what he had achieved as part of the team. As the project came to a successful end and he set off for home, he felt very happy indeed, not only because he had taken part in what had been built, but because he felt he had managed to 'leave home' in his mind. The experience made him feel, for the first time, that he could make the transition to university and manage his own life.

WHAT THE EXAMPLE SHOWS

Amir discovered through his personal experience that he could do something that he previously would not have thought possible. A process of internal growth took place. He took some time to find his way into the group, since he had to overcome feelings of jealousy before he could freely engage. But when he did, a whole new world of future possibilities – like leaving home and going to university – opened up to him.

SUMMARY

This chapter has suggested a way of thinking about your future plans in a rational way. It has also explained how dwelling too much on the future is not usually a good thing. It is a tricky balance to achieve – the future must not be ignored, but on the other hand it has to be treated as less important than the present. The key to achieving this balance is to develop the ability to use past and present experiences to expand and adapt your future plans.

AND FINALLY ... LETTING GO OF ADOLESCENCE

Many profound changes take place during adolescence. Relationships are made, broken and re-made. Your family adapts to your developing needs. You start to think about your career and take the first steps towards making it happen (making subject options at school, gaining work experience). Deep personal relationships may be made and the foundations laid down for a future life together. Issues are felt and responded to in a shatteringly deep or dramatic way.

Adolescence is a time of extremes – and for this reason it is both difficult to go through and, strangely, difficult to let it go. It may seem that things will never seem so intense, exciting or new again.

'Adolescence is a time of extremes – and, for this reason, it is both difficult to go through and, strangely, difficult to let it go.'

Letting go of adolescence also means taking responsibility for your own feelings in a way that is difficult at times during adolescence. We have come across examples in the case studies of people making those around them bear the brunt of their feelings. Leaving adolescence means recognising that you yourself are responsible for dealing with your own feelings. Hopefully the coping strategies you have learnt in this book will help you do this.

CHAPTER NINE:

NOT COPING
Making more use of yourself and others

This chapter will look at:

- The feeling of not coping
- Calling in extra help
- Professional help.

THE FEELING OF NOT COPING

It is normal to feel, from time to time, that you are not coping. It is important to be aware of the difference between this occasional and temporary feeling, which is connected to the number of things that are changing in your life, and another, more permanent feeling that you are in need of support.

What is not coping?

Normally this is about not being able to manage your life when another problem comes along. It may seem as if the latest thing is the last straw – as if you have no space for this new problem. But this is a quite normal response to change: there is usually going to be a tug of war between established ideas, and new ones.

Remember the questions we asked in the Introduction:

❏ **Are you adaptable?**
  Do you manage to think about new situations and adopt a flexible
  approach, or do you find it difficult to change your mind? Do you
  get caught up in routines that can't be changed?

❏ **Are you resilient?**
  What happens to you when something goes badly? Do you give up,
  or can you bounce back?

Sometimes these qualities alone seem as if they are not enough and
we feel we need extra support.

CALLING IN EXTRA HELP

Extra help can include:

■ Turning inwards
■ Turning outwards: parents/friends.

Turning inwards

Sometimes it turns out that the extra support we are looking for is
already there inside us. There are wonderful examples of the
unexpected resources that can be found inside us in the Harry Potter
books, particularly *The Prisoner of Azkaban*.

If you've read the book you may remember that at one point Harry
was very much at the mercy of the 'dementors', and it seemed

*'Sometimes it turns out that the extra
support we are looking for is already
there inside us.'*

inevitable that his spirit would be sucked from him. At the last moment, a 'patronus' (in the form of a unicorn) appears and banishes the Dementors.

It is interesting that Harry's first reaction is to think of the 'patronus' as a visit from his father to protect him. It is only later that he realises that it is not created by his father, but by himself. It was a part of himself that he did not know he had until he summoned it up, in desperation.

One way to think about this is to see the dementors as representing the negative thoughts in our minds, criticising us and dwelling on our faults. The effect of being sabotaged from within is to feel very weak, defenceless and depressed.

It seems that the word 'patronus' is derived from the Latin word 'pater', which means father. Like a parent, the Patronus can restore our strength by fighting on our behalf against a self-destructive side of ourselves.

The ability to turn inwards, when in crisis, is very important. It is connected to a couple of the general 'rules' mentioned in the Introduction:

❑ Self-regard: Are you kind in the way you think about yourself? Or are you self-critical, too harsh with yourself?
❑ Are you aware of your own feelings? Are you able to let your own feelings be felt, and expressed when appropriate? Or do you get too embarrassed, push feelings down, and pretend they are not there?

Turning outwards: parents/friends

As well as turning inwards towards our own resources, it is also very important to be able to look away from ourselves to other people.

PARENTS

It is normal during adolescence to find it difficult to talk things through with adults and it can be hard for adults to find the right words. It can be frustrating if this situation makes it impossible to talk to your parents when you need their help. If you need to talk urgently you might find you end up being lectured on room-tidying! If this happens, you need to explain calmly that there are other things on your mind than your dirty socks! Of course there is also the possibility that a dirty room may be linked to a depressed state of mind! Everyone needs access to a parental figure – but this figure does not actually have to be one of your parents; it can be any adult who you trust and respect, and who trusts and respects you.

'It is normal during adolescence to find it difficult to talk things through with adults ...'

FRIENDS

This might seem an easier way of relieving your problems. We discussed group membership in Chapter 3, and described how members of groups seem to be able to help each other face up to important issues by attaching different themes to individuals. We looked at the example of Ruth (the thin one), Sylvia (the talkative one), Tom (the lazy one) and Donna (in her own world). Groups can attract a mixture of different characters like this and this can enable you, as a member of the group, to look at and listen to someone else who has the same kind of problems that you are worried about. If you belong to a group you will be able to use this to do some reflecting on your own situation, rather than simply feel relieved that someone else also has the problem!

There are other group situations in which the members may not be associated with different themes in as rigid a way as that described, but can take up different roles in a flexible way.

PROFESSIONAL HELP

Sometimes friends and family or your own internal resources are not enough to enable you to cope. If this is the case then you may benefit from professional help. The list below gives some signals to look out for:

1 A worry has been with you a long time, and even if you get rid of it for a while, it comes back. You find it difficult to concentrate or make decisions.

2 You are behaving in an uncharacteristic way, eg short-tempered when you are usually patient, etc.

3 You are developing physical signs of stress, such as headaches, backaches or stomach-aches that don't go away.

4 You have recently had a stressful event, such as the break-up of a relationship, illness or bereavement.

What to make of the list?

It is important to keep it in perspective. It is possible to feel all of the above at some time, and the anxiety can pass away quite naturally. However, if you've been experiencing three out of four at the same time and for a while, this is an indication that help is needed.

What kind of help?

It is best to start with familiar places. For example, your school may have access to a counsellor who could help you. Different schools have different arrangements for supporting their students, and you should find that they provide you with posters, leaflets or other information and guidance on how to get help. If in doubt, your form tutor is a good place to start – ask to talk to them in confidence and explain the problems you are having.

Another option is to make an appointment to see your local doctor (GP). You could ask someone to do this for you, or look up their number in a telephone directory. GPs now have good links with new 'outreach' services in primary care and with Child and Adolescent Mental Health Services (CAMHS) which offer counselling services.

There is also a list of useful organisations at the end of this book.

As a general rule, it is best to start with the kind of help that will make it possible for you to talk about things that you are keeping inside too much. It is a common and ordinary worry to feel that you won't find someone who will be able to listen properly to what you are saying. A counsellor or therapy practitioner will be able to work with you and help you gain access to thoughts, feelings and plans for the future that it may not have been possible to do on your own.

'A counsellor or therapy practitioner will be able to work with you and help you gain access to thoughts, feelings and plans for the future that it may not have been possible to do on your own.'

SUMMARY

In this chapter we have looked at the ordinary feeling of not coping, which is often associated with change, and also at those times when additional help is needed. Although each form of help covered in the chapter has been presented separately, they can of course all be taking place at the same time: coping with change; becoming aware of your own internal resources; using a group or your family for support; and working with a counsellor.

CHAPTER TEN:

CONCLUSION
You and coping

The world changes so quickly and life is sometimes so complex that it's hardly surprising if we find it hard to cope at times. Adolescence, in particular, is a time when changes – physical, emotional, sexual, social – can sometimes seem overwhelming. We need to be able to recognise change and to accept that it is an inevitable part of life; and self-awareness, adaptability and resilience can help us get through times of change and upheaval.

Relationships change, too: with friends, parents, siblings. Close friendships are important: they can help us cope with life in general and can give us insights into our own feelings and ways of relating to other people. Being part of a group can be supportive, too – but it can also be destructive, as we saw in the discussion of groups and gangs in Chapter 3. We need to be aware of our own individuality within the

'The world changes so quickly and life is sometimes so complex that it's hardly surprising if we find it hard to cope at times.'

group. And to do this, we need to have a sense of ourselves and our personal history. This is a step on the way to developing a healthy self-regard, which we looked at in Chapter 5. This self-regard, and a sense of individual responsibility, can help us prevent our routines and habits from becoming emotional 'crutches' that we depend on.

It is also important to look towards the future. Your own sense of yourself will help point you towards the future that you want and that is right for you.

In Chapter 9 we looked at not coping and discussed how to call on help from inside ourselves and from parents and friends: we also touched on professional help and when it might be needed. The checklist for coping given in the Introduction (on page 2) is worth referring back to when you're feeling you can't cope. It can help you define the problem and the way you are responding to it, and give you a basis for moving on.

In the final chapter of this book (Chapter 11) we will list some useful contacts and sources of further information, as well as recommending some interesting reading that may help you reflect on problems affecting your own life.

This has been a book about coping with life in general. We have made a number of comments about coping, which can be summarised as follows.

1 'Coping' in a general sense is not the same as coping brilliantly all the time.

2 A natural part of coping generally is to be able to respond to changes in your life.

3 There are broad rules about coping. In this book we have concentrated on the following:

■ having self-regard, being adaptable and being resilient

■ being aware of the company you keep, whether with individuals or groups

■ being aware of the roles that habits and routines of different kinds play in your life

■ being in touch with your mind and your feelings.

Good luck on your journey!

FURTHER
INFORMATION
*Brief reviews of
good books,
and contact
information for
useful
organisations*

SOMETHING TO READ

This section looks at a number of novels that deal with teenage experiences. These books may help you to reflect on issues in your own life, and to look at how different individuals respond to different situations. Each book raises powerful issues and none of them gives simple, cut-and-dried solutions – but then life rarely has simple, cut-and-dried solutions. Not all of the books will appeal to everyone, but they have been reviewed by teenagers who enjoyed them.

City of the Beasts by Isabel Allende (translated from the Spanish by Margaret Sayers Peden) (Flamingo, 2003)

'A boy's mother is in hospital. He goes to stay with his rather "scary" grandmother and they make a journey into the Amazon. He meets a

girl and has to go on a trek to save the people who live there from dangers of the world. It is about finding out who you are and having to grow up.'   **Carys**

Noughts and Crosses by Malorie Blackman (Corgi, 2002)

'A story of two teenagers growing up in a racist country. One is rich and black, the other white and poor. They try to remain friends though society is pushing them apart. It really makes you think. They have a rich relationship with each other.'   **Carys**

Walk Two Moons by Sharon Creech (Macmillan, 1995)

'Lovely, interesting and beautifully written. It deals with growing up, losing someone you love, and making new friends.'   **Carys**

Absolutely Normal Chaos by Sharon Creech (Macmillan, 1995)

'A teenage girl is asked to write a journal of her summer holidays. It is funny, entertaining and assures you that your family isn't the strangest in the world.'   **Carys**

Tales of Otori trilogy by Liam Hearn (Macmillan, 2004)
   Book One: *Across the Nightingale Floor*
   Book Two: *Grass for his Pillow*
   Book Three: *Brilliance of the Moon*

'Some of the most beautiful books I've ever read. Two teenagers living in ancient Japan have to grow up fast and become adults. It is an enormous story of love, courage and responsibility.'   **Owen**

***The Arthur Trilogy* by Kevin Crossley-Holland (Orion, 2001)**
The Seeing Stone
At the Crossing Places
King of the Middle March

*'A story, set in the Middle Ages, of a boy who gets a "seeing stone"
which shows him his life and what he will have to do. Very good, very
interesting.'*   **Owen**

***Journey to the River Sea* by Eva Ibbotson (Macmillan, 2001)**

*'A story of becoming older, but intertwined with a mystery plot as well
as teenage relationships!'*   **Rosie**

***Boy Kills Man* by Matt Whyman (Hodder, 2004)**

*'This is a powerful story, set in South America. Two friends, Shorty and
Alberto, are "blood brothers", just thirteen, trying to survive in a world
of guns and drugs. I was really struck by the violence of the world
they have to grow up in.'*   **Owen**

Other books

The following are all series that you might well be familiar with.

The *Circle of Magic* series, a fantasy quartet by Tamara Pierce
(Scholastic, 1998)
The Magic in the Weaving; *The Power in the Storm*; *The Fire in the
Forging*; *The Healing in the Vine*

His Dark Materials, a trilogy by Philip Pullman (Scholastic, 2000)
Northern Lights; *The Subtle Knife*; *The Amber Spyglass*

The Harry Potter series by J. K. Rowling (Bloomsbury, 2000)
The Philosopher's Stone; *The Chamber of Secrets*; *The Prisoner of Azkaban*; *The Goblet of Fire; The Half-Blood Prince* (incomplete series)

A series of books by Jacqueline Wilson, including *Girls in Love*; *Girls under Pressure*; *Girls out Late*; *Girls in Tears* (Corgi, 2003)

Happy reading!

USEFUL ORGANISATIONS & WEBSITES

Adfam www.adfam.org.uk
Waterbridge House
32–36 Loman Street
London SE1 0EH
Tel: 020 7928 8898
Advice for families facing problems with drugs or alcohol.

Anti-Bullying Campaign www.bullying.co.uk
185 Tower Bridge Road
London SE1 2UF
Tel: 020 7378 1446
Advice for victims of bullying and their parents.

Brook Advisory Services www.brook.org.uk
421 Highgate Studios
53–79 Highgate Road
London NW5 1TL
Tel: 020 7284 6040
Helpline: 020 7617 8000 (24 hours a day)
Confidential advice on sexual health and contraception for young people.

ChildLine www.childline.org.uk
45 Folgate Street
London E1 6GL
Tel: 020 7650 3200
Helpline: 0800 1111 (for children and young people)
Confidential 24-hour helpline for children and young people.

Eating Disorders Association www.edauk.com
103 Prince of Wales Road
Norwich, Norfolk NR1 1DW
Helpline: 0160 362 1414 (Monday to Friday 9 am to 6:30 pm)
Youthline: 0160 376 5050 (Monday to Friday 4 pm to 6 pm)
Information on all aspects of eating disorders.

Get Connected www.getconnected.org.uk
Freephone: 0808 808 4994 (7 days a week 1 pm to 11 pm)
Finds young people the best available help, whatever the problem. Puts you in touch with organisations that can help.

Gingerbread Association for One-Parent Families
www.gingerbread.org.uk
7 Sovereign Close
London E1W 2HW
Tel: 020 7488 9300
Advice Line: 0800 018 4318 (Monday to Friday 9 am to 5 pm)
Support for single-parent families.

Release www.release.org.uk
388 Old Street
London EC1V 9LT
Tel: 020 7729 9904
Helpline: 0845 450 0215
Information on drugs, the law and human rights.

Samaritans www.samaritans.org.uk
The Upper Mill, Kingston Road
Ewell, Surrey KT17 2AF
Tel: 020 8394 8300
Helpline: 0845 790 9090 (24 hours a day)
Confidential emotional support for people experiencing feelings of distress and despair, or contemplating suicide.

Turning Point www.turning-point.co.uk
101 Backchurch Lane
London E1 1LU
Tel: 020 7702 2300
Services for people with complex needs, including drug and alcohol misuse, mental health problems and learning disabilities.

YoungMinds/National Association for Child and Family Mental Health www.youngminds.org.uk
102–108 Clerkenwell Road
London EC1M 5SA
Tel: 020 7336 8445
Parents' Information Service: 0800 018 2138
Campaign to improve the mental health of children and young people.

Youthnet www.youthnet.co.uk
A website for young people that covers a range of different topics.

USEFUL BOOKS

Trotman's Real Life Issues series

Self-help books offering information and advice on a range of key issues that matter to you. Each book defines the issue, and offers ways of understanding and coping with it. Real Life Issues aim to demystify the areas that you might find hard to talk about, providing honest facts, practical advice, inspirational quotes and firm reassurance. The following titles are available from Trotman Publishing, Tel: 0870 900 2665:

Addictions, Stephen Briggs
Bullying, Emma Caprez
Confidence & Self-Esteem, Nicki Household
Eating Disorders, Heather Warner
Money, Dee Pilgrim
Sex & Relationships, Adele Cherreson Cole
Stress, Rozina Breen

Young Minds

The Young Minds website has a very good list of resources and further reading material on a huge range of areas – from coping with bereavement, pressure, depression or divorce to anger management, being an in-patient and getting help from social services. They are all listed on the Reading and resources page of their website: www.youngminds.org.uk/youngpeople/reading.php.

trotman

Supportive, friendly and informative

REAL LIFE ISSUES:

Addictions
Bullying
Confidence & Self-Esteem
Coping with Life

Eating Disorders
Money
Sex and Relationships
Stress

For more details or to buy any of these titles, visit
www.trotman.co.uk

trotman

THE
'WINNING'
SERIES

Winning
CVs for
First-Time
Job Hunters

Winning
Interviews
for First-Time
Job Hunters

Winning
Job-Hunting
Strategies
for First-Time
Job Hunters

Do you need help with applying for that all-important first full/part-time job or work experience placement? The *Winning* series will guide you through the often-daunting process of finding work and will provide you with the confidence you need to get the job you want.

FOR MORE DETAILS OR TO BUY ANY OF THESE TITLES VISIT WWW.TROTMAN.CO.UK